harmless

Study Guide

Ana Verhar

Flying Pig Press

www.flyingpigpress.ch

Harmless Study Guide
Ana Verhar

ISBN 978-3-033-02213-3

Note: Page references in this study guide are based on the 2007 Wendy Lamb Books hardcover edition of *Harmless* by Dana Reinhardt, ISBN 978-0-385-74699-1. The Wendy Lamb Books paperback edition of 2008, ISBN 978-0-553-49497-6, has the same page numbers.

Words have power. Not like engines, like atoms.
You can split your whole life apart
if you gather all the wrong words together in the right place.

-- Taylor Mali, *The wisest woman in the eighth grade*

Contents

Aims

The primary aim of this study guide is for students to gain in-depth understanding of Dana Reinhardt's novel *Harmless*. Further aims are to engage students' curiosity, to provide a basis for discussion which motivates students to think critically about interpersonal dynamics and ethics, to develop students' awareness of literary devices and their effects and go beyond superficial understanding of mere plot and thus allow students to grow through their reading and critical reflection of literature. All activities in this study guide are designed to further students' writing, speaking, critical and analytical thinking skills, as well as their imagination and creativity. The wide range of activities and exercises offers teachers opportunities for varied assessment.

As Dana Reinhardt's novel *Harmless* is recommended for readers in grades 7-10, so is this study guide. It can be used with native speakers or learners of English at an at least intermediate level. Teachers of native speakers might choose to focus mainly on literary elements, graphic organizers, writing tasks and use comprehension questions and vocabulary exercises as a means to ensure that the novel has been read. Teachers of learners of English on the other hand might focus on using particularly the main part of the study guide and vocabulary exercises to assist students in their reading of an unabridged literary text and boost their confidence by using the questions to let them experience how much they in fact understand without understanding every word. This should make the reading an enjoyable instead of frightening experience. The study guide can also accommodate a layered curriculum if teachers choose to assign different tasks to different students and/ or have students of different skill levels complete tasks jointly in cooperative learning activities. Aims, teaching methods, order of assigning tasks and sections in or out of class, expected or required quality of responses and assessment will naturally vary and be determined by the age and competence of the student as well as the school's curriculum policies.

Structure

This study guide includes a wide range of activities and exercises, divided into a pre-reading part, a graphic organizer part that offers an overview of the text, a main part working closely with the text, a graphic organizer part meant to gain deeper insight into characters and interpersonal dynamics, and a text composition part. Many task formats are recurrent to help students know what to expect and experience progress, while some offer variation to fit the demands of the text or build up skills to complete progressively challenging assignments.

Teachers can assign the respective tasks in each section in their order of preference and / or use sections for different types of assessment. The study guide offers single-task assignments to be completed as a one-time event in class or as homework, but also tasks that can be worked on continuously. For instance graphic organizers such as the Text Components Factsheet, the Plot Map, or the character diagrams in the second graphic organizer part can be assigned either as a continuous task as the reading progresses, or as a summing-up-activity or even a test of students' analytical skills after the novel has been read.

Pre-reading tasks encourage students to anticipate developments, discuss expectations, and find convincing arguments to back up claims and opinions in written and spoken form. Graphic organizers teach students to structure information visually, and thus develop strategies to identify similarities, differences, relationships, conflicts, interpersonal dynamics, and narrative structures.

The study guide's main part is structured in seven sections based on reading assignments of roughly 40 pages from Dana Reinhardt's novel *Harmless*. Each reading section includes a summary task, vocabulary exercises, text comprehension or discussion questions and novel-based writing tasks. The summary tasks help students capture the main elements of the plot while reinforcing their awareness of the unique narrative structure of the novel. Vocabulary activities ensure the comprehension of some pivotal words used in the novel and thus enrich and expand students' vocabulary. Vocabulary exercises include sentence completion tasks (clozes), mix-and-match tasks, understanding and training of idioms and parts of speech, writing own sentences and miniature stories using select words from the novel. Writing tasks and the "How-to-Write" part introduce different text types (see list below) and strategies of text composition such as paragraphing, supporting an argument, using transitions, considering subject, purpose, audience and registers, etc. Reading comprehension and discussion questions demand students to pay close attention to developments and construction of plot, characters, dialogue and phrasing, and require exact reading, careful contemplation and scrutiny of the text.

List of Text-Type-Specific Writing Tasks

Pre-Reading Tasks

Think about the following statements and rate them on a scale of 1-4 (strongly agree (4) to strongly disagree (1)). In few keywords, briefly justify your stance for each statement.

Statement	Rating	Keyword Justification
Sometimes it is easier to tell lies than it is to tell the truth.	**1 2 3 4**	
A 14-year old teenager knows the difference between right and wrong.	**1 2 3 4**	
Beggars and homeless people should not be allowed on the street.	**1 2 3 4**	
Teenagers should not have sex.	**1 2 3 4**	
Truth hurts.	**1 2 3 4**	
Public school is for losers.	**1 2 3 4**	
Becoming an adult means taking responsibility for your actions.	**1 2 3 4**	
Certain things cannot be forgiven.	**1 2 3 4**	
Lies can be helpful.	**1 2 3 4**	
If no one knows that I have done something wrong I do not feel guilty about it.	**1 2 3 4**	
The best part about having a boy/girlfriend is that you can show him/her off to others.	**1 2 3 4**	
If you cannot talk about everything you are not real friends.	**1 2 3 4**	
Everybody tells lies.	**1 2 3 4**	
Boys and girls cannot be just friends.	**1 2 3 4**	
All teenage boys can think of is sex.	**1 2 3 4**	
Lying is pointless because the truth always comes out sooner or later.	**1 2 3 4**	

Only parents who cannot handle their children send them to boarding school.	**1 2 3 4**	
In some situations there is no clear distinction between what is right and what is wrong.	**1 2 3 4**	
If you have a boy/girlfriend you are more popular.	**1 2 3 4**	
My parents expect too much from me.	**1 2 3 4**	
Children from good homes are less likely to commit criminal acts than children from dysfunctional homes.	**1 2 3 4**	
All teenage girls can think of is sex.	**1 2 3 4**	
Most homeless people are criminals or crazies.	**1 2 3 4**	
If someone apologizes about something he should be forgiven.	**1 2 3 4**	
You should only have sex with someone you truly love.	**1 2 3 4**	
I love to be at the center of attention.	**1 2 3 4**	
I would rather be punished than hurt someone else with my actions.	**1 2 3 4**	
You should tell the truth at all costs.	**1 2 3 4**	
Teenagers older than 14 should be treated and punished as adults.	**1 2 3 4**	
Sometimes it's easier to talk to a stranger than to close friends or parents.	**1 2 3 4**	
Teenage boys should not date girls who are 3 or more years younger than they are.	**1 2 3 4**	
Lies destroy you.	**1 2 3 4**	
Boarding school gives children a better chance to be independent from their parents.	**1 2 3 4**	

From the above statements choose **three** that you feel most strongly about. Write one paragraph (7-10 sentences) to explain and defend your stance regarding each of those three statements. Prepare to give a 3 minute presentation explaining your reaction to class.

Text Components – Factsheet

Keyword-question	Answer / Explanation / Justification
Author	
Narrator	
Point-of-view	
Genre	
Setting	
Protagonist	
Antagonist	
3 main conflicts	
Purpose or message of book	
Most memorable	
What you liked best	
What you liked the least	
What you have learned	

Plot Map

Complete the plot map below by writing the corresponding events in the boxes. Justify your choice of events.

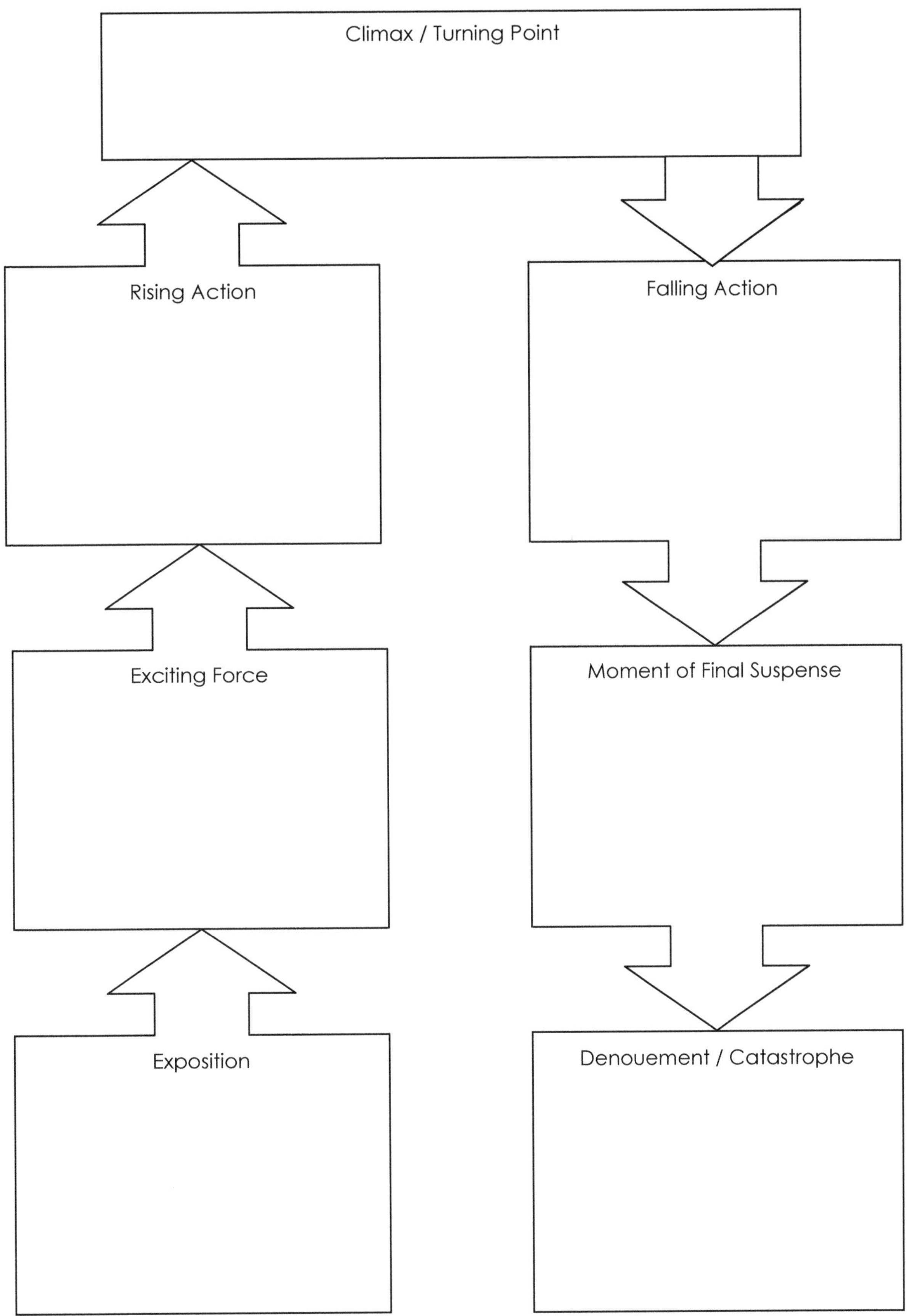

Section 1 : *Harmless* pages 1-12

Questions

1. How does the opening of the very first chapter create suspense or expectations?

2. What does the opening of the very first chapter suggest about truth?

3. What do the headings of the first three chapters suggest about the narrative technique used in this book?

4. What is the effect of this narrative technique?

5. What does Anna find appealing about Mariah?

6. What does Anna believe "hanging out" means?

7. What does Anna mean by "I could see why a guy like Romeo might kill himself over her" (4) ?

8. To what does Emma compare living in a small town? Why?

9. Do you agree? Why yes, why not?

10. Write a paragraph explaining why you would prefer to live in a small town or a big city.

11. As Anna introduces the story, what seems to be most important to her to communicate to the reader?

12. As Emma introduces the story, what seems to be most important to her to communicate to the reader?

13. As Mariah introduces the story, what seems to be most important to her to communicate to the reader?

14. What do these respective interests tell about the personality of these girls?

Vocabulary

Use the words from the novel printed in the cloud to complete the sentences in the box. Be careful to use the correct form of verbs, and the plural or singular form of nouns.

threaten, resolution, windowsill, gasp, dorky, ache, irresponsible, assignment, devotion, yard, cage, shortage, ordinary, dimple, twirl, adjust, broaden, pudgy, blame, sparkle, slut, impress, freckles, brag, conduct, hickey, give someone the time of day, give … an edge, wince, itchy, sip

1. A ______________ is a mark left on your skin by passionate kissing.
2. You ______________ if you struggle to breathe.
3. I have a huge crush on Tom, but he ignores me completely. Tom just won't give me ______________.
4. We do not have enough food for everyone: there is a ______________ of food.
5. Her good looks gave Saundra an ______________ in the interview – she had a clear advantage over some of the less appealing applicants.
6. Tony's clothes are very old-fashioned and he's only interested in school. He is __________.
7. If something hurts we can also say that it ______________.
8. If your body draws back or tenses as if from a physical blow, we say that you __________.
9. Something ______________ needs to be scratched.
10. To __________ something means to spin or rotate it rapidly around an axis.
11. After being pregnant I had to ______________ my clothes so they fit me again.
12. There is nothing special about Pedro. He is an ______________ person.
13. Another word for a garden or area surrounding a house is the __________.
14. If you indicate to someone that there will be severe consequences to his actions if he doesn't do as you wish, then you ______________ that person.
15. Animals in a zoo are often kept in very small ______________ with iron bars.
16. A task you have to complete for school is called an ______________.
17. My New Year's ______________ is to stop smoking and improve my grades: I have decided to do this and will work hard to achieve it.
18. If you want to ______________ your knowledge you should try to read a great variety of books so your knowledge expands.
19. Babies are often ______________: they have short limbs with lots of baby-fat.
20. When you smile, the soft parts of your face might create a funny little hollow: a ______________.
21. Many people think that wearing expensive brandname clothing will ______________ other people. If you show off your money in such a way, you ______________.
22. The little brown spots in your face, usually caused by the sun, are called ______________.
23. I knew that it was Peter's fault that I did not pass my test. I ______________ Peter for my bad grade.
24. A profound attachment to a person or the worshipping of a god is called ______________.
25. A brilliant gem might glisten or ______________ in the light.
26. The horizontal part at the base of a window's opening is the ______________.
27. I'm not thirsty, but would like to taste this cocktail. Can I have a ______________ from your glass?
28. When you meet the president your ______________ should be above reprimand: you must not behave foolishly or wear a bikini.
29. Leaving his friend alone in the snowstorm showed what an ______________ person Oliver was.
30. A person who is considered sexually promiscuous is informally called a ______________.

Section 2 : *Harmless* pages 13-48

Summary

Write a summary of the events that occur in this reading section. Distinguish between the parts of the story told by Anna, Emma, and Mariah.

Vocabulary

Use the words from the novel printed in the cloud to complete the sentences in the box. Be careful to use the correct form of verbs, and the plural or singular form of nouns.

peel whisper
hurt notice immediately
hint whistle obey miscarriage
bottom façade secret tear
skin
huge command joy envelope fend
curly surface siblings complain
basement invisible attention
order hesitate

1. If you get someone's attention, that person ____________________ you.
2. A person who cannot be seen is _________________________.
3. If someone causes you pain, that person ____________________ you.
4. When you pull a piece of paper apart many times, you _____________________ it to pieces.
5. You do not want anyone to overhear what you are saying, so you speak in a very low voice: you ____________________.
6. Before you post a letter you have to put it in an _______________________.
7. Great delight or happiness is called _________________.
8. If a baby is born either dead or so prematurely that it cannot survive, we speak of a ______________.
9. Your brothers and sisters are your ___________________.
10. The opposite of straight hair is ____________________ hair.
11. His deliberate cough caught the waiter's _____________________.
12. The room underneath your house is the ______________________.
13. You are dissatisfied with the meal served at the restaurant because there was a hair in your soup and salt instead of sugar in your desert, so you march into the kitchen and ______________________.
14. Every person has a __________________: something we do not want anyone else to know.
15. Page numbers in this study guide can be found at the _________________ of the page.
16. If something is very big it can be called ________________.
17. A referee in a soccer match will ___________________ to get the attention of the players.
18. The outside or uppermost part of something is the ______________. As a verb, the word means to rise up.
19. The front of a building or superficial appearance of something is its __________________.
20. Before you eat an orange, you need to _________________ it: you strip it of its skin.
21. If you do not want to go out to eat or cook yourself, you can __________________ pizza.
22. If you follow an order you ________________.
23. If you order someone to do something, you ___________________ that person.
24. If something happens at once and without delay, it happens _____________________.
25. The external covering of our body is our ____________________.
26. If I give you a helpful suggestion or clue, I give you a _________________.
27. If you have doubts or are afraid of making a decision you __________________.
28. Don't worry about Tom, he can ___________________ for himself. He will find a way to manage any situation on his own.

Vocabulary : Idioms and Parts of Speech

Use the words from the novel printed in the banner to complete the sentences. For each word indicate its part of speech (noun, verb, adjective, or adverb) as used in the sentence by writing it on top of the box. Supply an additional part of speech of the same word if prompted.

An idiom is an expression that cannot be understood from the literal meanings of individual words. For example the expression *It's raining cats and dogs* does not mean that cats and dogs are falling from the sky, but suggests that it is raining very heavily. The origin of idioms is not always clear. This one may come from Norse mythology where cats were supposed to have an influence over the weather, while dogs were the signal of storms. It is often difficult for people learning English to understand its many idiomatic expressions. To practice understanding and using idioms, first use a word printed in the banner to complete the sentence that explains its literal meaning. Then try to explain what the idiom using that word might mean.

assume partial roof adult pride mature closet fail

1. If you do not succeed you ______. Noun: ______

2. If something is incomplete it is ______. Noun: ______

Idiom: I am partial to chocolate. Possible explanation:

3. The opposite of a child is an ______. Careful! Do not mix up reaching adulthood with *adultery* which means that you are cheating on your husband or wife.

4. If a fruit is ripe, or a person has fully developed in body and mind, we call it ______.

Noun: ______ Verb: ______

5. A small storage room or cabinet is a ______.

Idiom: to be in the closet means:

to come out of the closet means:

6. Having a high opinion of one's achievements is known as ______.

Adjective: ______

7. It is never good to suppose something without proof, particularly if we ______ the worst about a person or event. Noun: ______

8. The external covering of the top of a house is its ______.

Idiom: to hit the roof means:

Vocabulary

Match these words from the novel with their definitions by writing the correct number on the line. Choose ten words and write one sentence per word in which you use the word correctly and show that you have understood its meaning. Indicate the part of speech of the word as used in the sentence.

1. bribe
2. bangs
3. tomboy
4. harsh
5. loyal
6. captivity
7. generic
8. suggest
9. hide
10. establish
11. loner
12. avoid
13. host
14. stranger
15. honest
16. awkward
17. trust
18. odious
19. admit
20. ridiculous
21. standing ovations
22. campus
23. suspicious
24. permission
25. opportunity
26. gorgeous
27. criticize
28. clueless
29. wrath
30. occupied
31. slice
32. dare
33. yawn
34. pretend
35. absentminded
36. flushed
37. crush
38. muscular
39. bracelet
40. mumble
41. unpleasant
42. retreat

___ to acknowledge or confess
___ laughable or worthy of derision
___ an intense but short-lived passion for someone
___ having a well-developed body
___ to rely on
___ to prevent from being seen or discovered
___ busy, filled up
___ to speak indistinctly, as with partly closed lips
___ A fringe of hair combed over the forehead
___ splendid, magnificent, highly enjoyable in appearance
___ withdraw, move backwards defensively
___ to deceive or make believe
___ truthful
___ fierce anger
___ a person who avoids the company of others
___ a girl whose behavior and interests are considered more typical of boys
___ money or promise of something valuable to corrupt a person's behavior to one's own benefit
___ common or ordinary
___ hard to deal with, uncomfortable
___ jewelry you wear around your wrist
___ a thin, flat piece cut from something
___ to judge and find fault
___ questionable and distrustful
___ the grounds of a school
___ to keep away from, to shun
___ to have the courage or boldness for something, to challenge
___ lacking understanding or knowledge
___ authorization to do something
___ ungentle, very strict, rough, or severe
___ An audience will show its enthusiasm and respect by applauding while standing up.
___ faithful and aware of one's obligations
___ hateful, detestable, disgusting
___ to found or settle in a position
___ to propose or bring up for consideration
___ a person who receives and entertains guests
___ to open the mouth for an intake of air, often due to fatigue or boredom
___ the state of being imprisoned, held, confined
___ a person with whom one is not acquainted
___ preoccupied to the extent of being unaware of one's surroundings
___ chance
___ disagreeable
___ to turn red as from fever or strong emotion

Questions

1. Anna is no stranger to lying. Which little lies has she been told, which lies has she told herself and why?

2. What is the difference between a lie and a half-truth? (14)

3. Look at the online profile Mariah suggests Carl should have written. What does this illustrate about their relationship? About Carl as a person? Is Mariah a reliable source of information about Carl?

4. Write the online profile Carl really wrote.

5. Why does Mariah want Emma or Anna to start dating one of her boyfriend's friends? What does this show about her?

6. Anna claims on page 27 that she had never lied to her parents before. Is that true?

7. Anna claims that "figuring out your own way through the world means lying to your parents"(30). Do you agree? Explain your answer.

8. What story did the 6th grade science teacher tell to scare students off drugs? Do you think that this story discourages teenagers from trying drugs? Why yes, why not?

9. What nickname does Emma give her brother Silas? What does this suggest?

10. What does Emma mean by saying "The privileged world of those who have boyfriends closed its iron doors to me" (36).

11. Emma speaks about a double standard in her family. What does she mean? Have you experienced similar double standards? Give examples.

12. Emma claims that "parents don't really want to know the truth"(37). Do you agree?

13. Mariah describes her sexual experiences with DJ. What do you find surprising about them? What does how she tells us about them show about her personality?

14. What does Mariah do once she and her girlfriends arrive at DJ's house? Would you have done the same? Why yes, why not?

15. Why does Mariah find it easy to lie?

16. What does DJ say that quiets Mariah into believing that "there was nothing more for me to say" (43) ? Why do you think she believes this?

17. How do you expect Mariah, Anna, and Emma to behave at the party?

18. What surprises you about Anna's and Emma's behavior at the party?

19. What do you think Anna saw when she woke up in the middle of the night?

20. Which of the three girls do you like best? Which do you like the least? Explain your likes and dislikes in 2 paragraphs. Use at least 7 words from the banner below in your writing.

whereas	similarly	additionally	nevertheless	despite	in contrast
although	therefore	such as	on the one hand	on the other hand	
for example	in particular	consequently	this is why	most importantly	
especially	first of all	to begin with	next	in conclusion	

Section 3 : *Harmless* pages 49-73

Summary

Write a summary of the events that occur in this reading section. Distinguish between the parts of the story told by Anna, Emma, and Mariah.

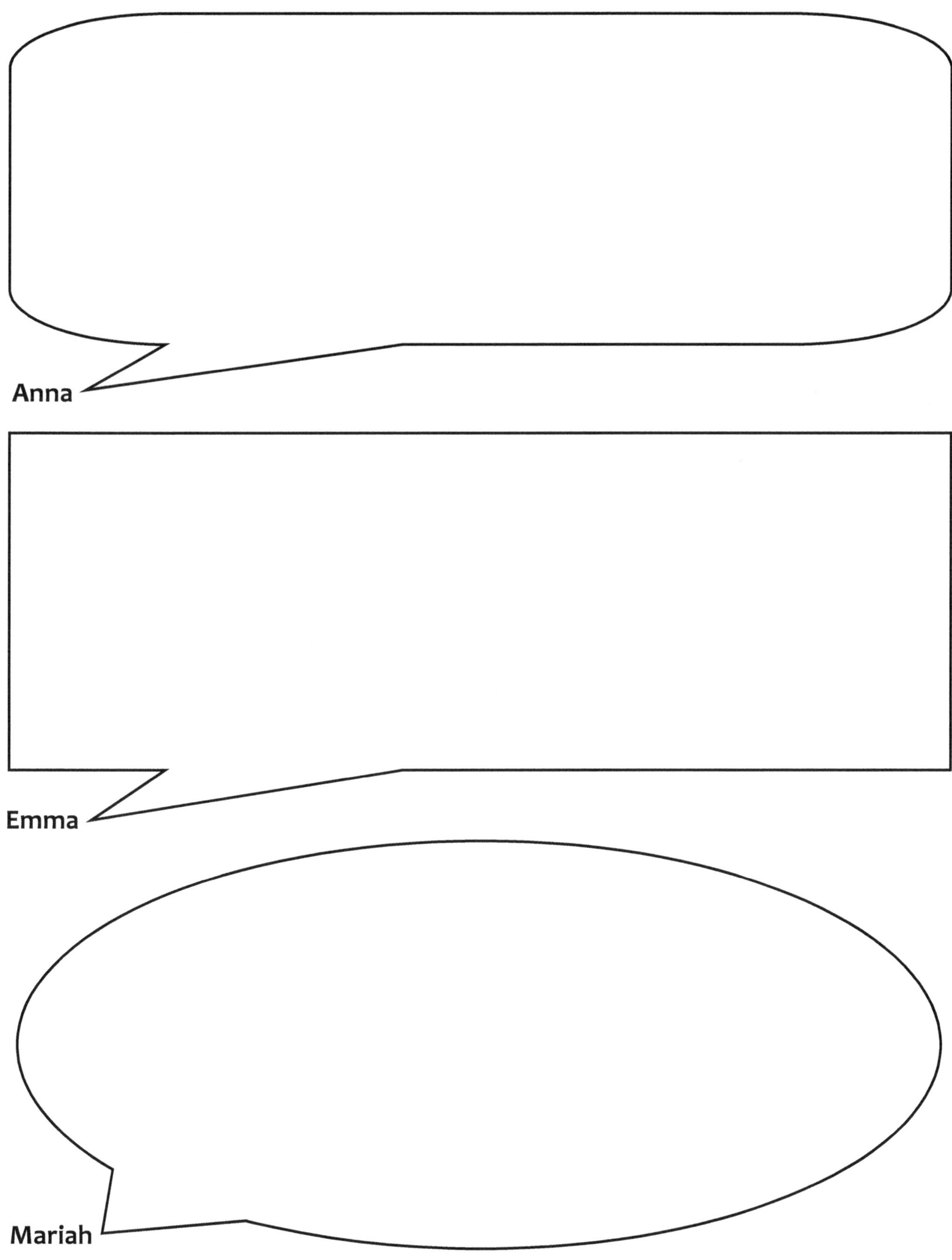

Vocabulary

Determine the part of speech of the words from the novel printed in the cloud. Use these words or one of their parts of speech to complete the sentences in the box. Be careful to use the correct form of verbs, and the plural or singular form of nouns.

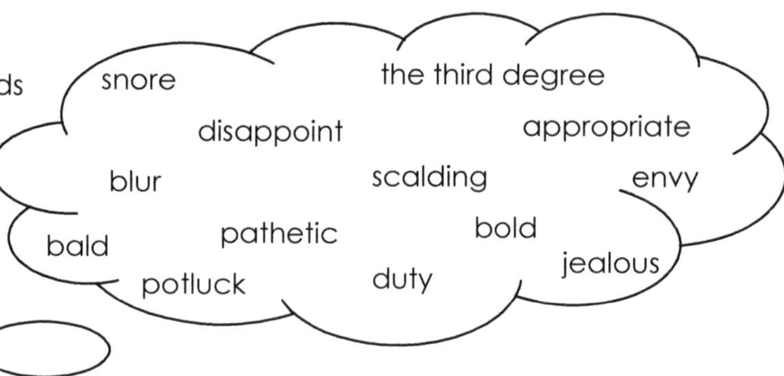

1. If you fail to fulfill the hopes, wishes, or expectations of someone you ____________________ that person.
2. The popular definition of the word ____________________ is something miserably inadequate or pitiable. The original definition of the word goes back to the Greek word *pathos* and suggests something grand that causes great emotion.
3. A ____________________ is a meal to which participants bring various foods to be shared.
4. If something is hot to the boiling point it is ____________________.
5. You cannot wear a bikini to Christmas Dinner but should appear ____________________ dressed for the occasion.
6. This word describes a feeling of discontent and resentment aroused by the desire for the possessions of another person. For example, I ____________________ Alex for driving a Ferrari. If I resent a person for spending time with or getting attention from a person that I particularly like, I am ____________________.
7. Something that you are expected or required to do by moral or legal obligation is your ______________.
8. Some people make loud grunting sounds in their sleep: they ____________________.
9. When something is obscured or confused in its form or outline it is ____________________.
10. Giving someone ____________________ means to question that person roughly and remain suspicious about the truthfulness of his answers.
11. Another word for brave or courageous is ____________________. Do not confuse this word with the word ____________________ which means that someone has no hair left on his head.

Vocabulary

Match these words from the novel with their definitions by writing the correct number on the line.

1. drag
2. insignificant
3. contemplate
4. reflect
5. crouch
6. sassy
7. purge
8. predict
9. circumstance
10. hurry
11. sob

___ to bend close to the ground, either in preparation to attack, or in fear
___ rude and disrespectful
___ unimportant
___ tell something in advance
___ to cast back light or an image, to give a particular impression
___ to move with haste
___ clear, purify, cleanse, get rid of something undesirable
___ to think fully or deeply about
___ the sound made when crying and catching your breath
___ the conditions or state of affairs surrounding and affecting a person or event
___ to pull heavily and trail along the ground

Choose five words from above and write one sentence per word in which you use the word correctly and show that you have understood its meaning. Indicate the part of speech of the word as used in the sentence.

Example: At an auction items are sold by public outcry to the highest bidder.
(noun)

Questions

1. Why do you think Emma feels filthy despite taking a shower?

2. What does Emma mean by "it was so much simpler in the grammatical days of Michael Landau"(52) ?

3. Write down the simile Emma uses on page 54 to describe her feelings after the night of the party. Explain what she might mean by this.

4. Why does Mariah believe she is a genius? Do you agree?

5. According to Mariah, what is Carl very concerned about?

6. What does Mariah mean by "he wanted me to be the Disney version of the perfect older sister" (57) ?

7. Why does Mariah envy Anna?

8. The relationship between the girls has changed after the party. Note the changes.

9. Anna tells us about some of Emma's secrets. How does Emma's past behavior shed light on her current behavior?

10. What does Emma want to do on Friday night? Why does she not do what she wants?

11. Which four important things happened on that Friday night?

12. Why is Mariah upset with DJ? What does this show about their relationship?

13. What does Emma mean by "I felt the sting of those words, sharp behind my eyes, aching in my body, my heart." (69)

14. What story do the girls concoct to tell their parents? Give a detailed answer.

15. Why do you think Emma suggests to tell that story?

16. What might be possible problems or holes in that story?

17. How would you as a parent react to this story?

18. How do you think will the respective parents of the girls react to the story?

Section 4 : *Harmless* pages 74-89

Summary

Write a summary of the events that occur in this reading section. Make sure your summary includes which consequences the telling of the story has for each girl.

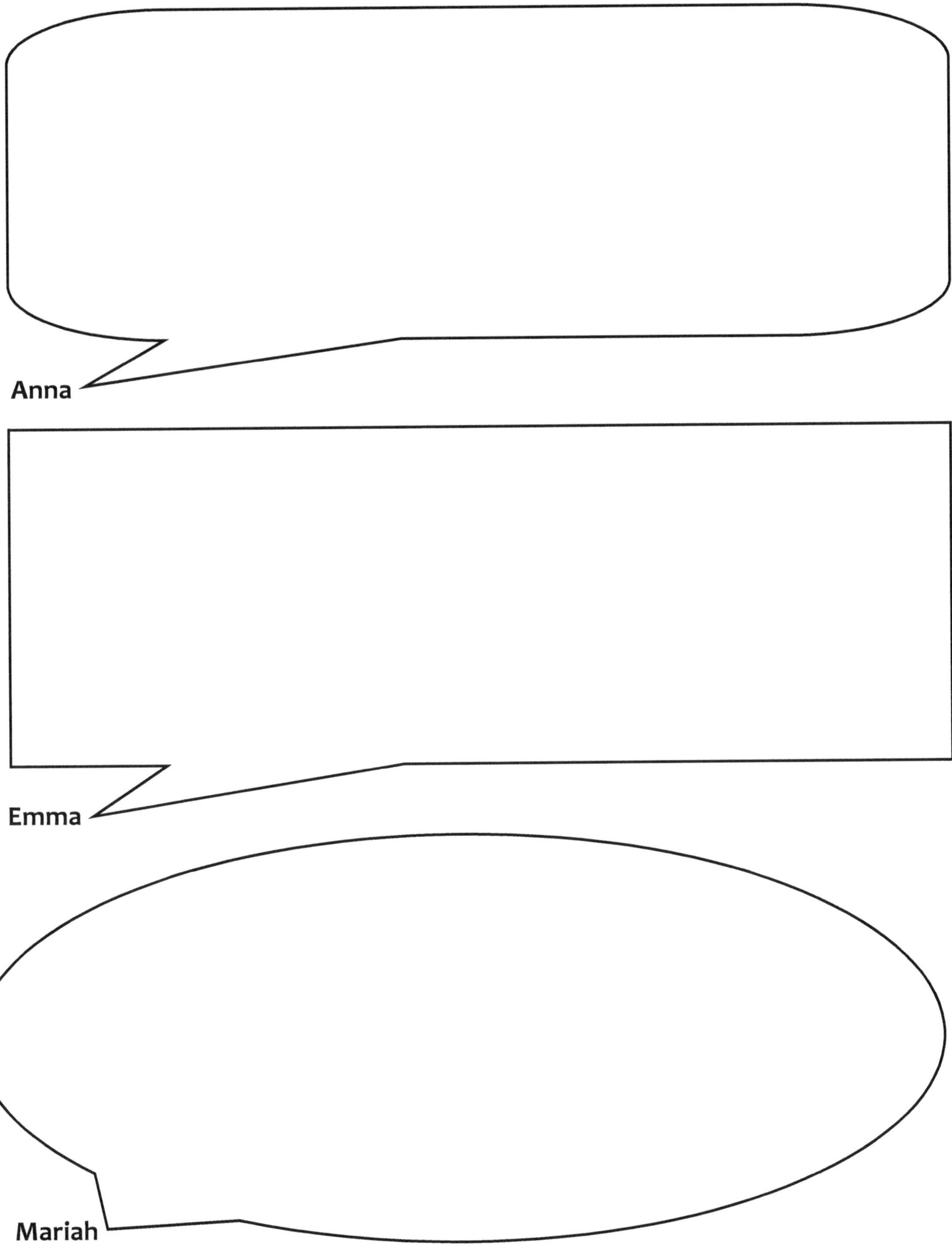

Reactions

Note the respective reactions to the telling of the story. Quote passages and give page references to back up your claims.

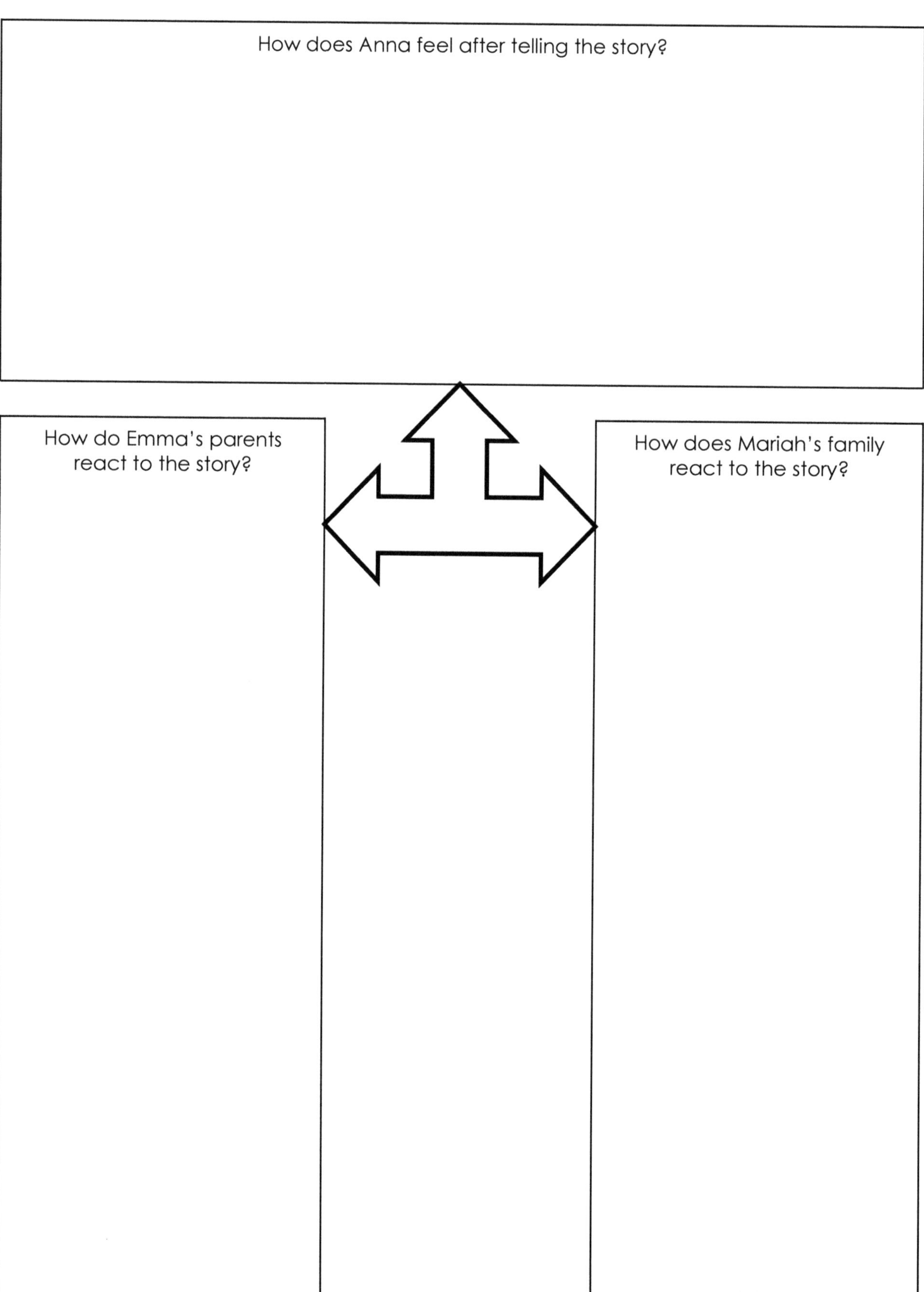

Vocabulary

Match these words from the novel with their definitions by writing the correct number on the line. For each word write one sentence in which you use the word correctly and show that you have understood its meaning. Indicate the part of speech of the word as used in the sentence.

1. skim
2. incident
3. lanky
4. vague
5. furious
6. response
7. insist
8. harm
9. disrupt
10. cancel

___ to stay firm in a demand or course
___ extremely angry
___ tall and very thin
___ to call off
___ to hurt
___ answer or reply in word or action
___ an event that is out of the ordinary and might cause a crisis
___ to read in a fast, superficial manner
___ to break apart, interrupt, or cause disorder
___ not clearly stated or explained

Example: At an auction items are sold by public outcry to the highest bidder.
(noun)

Section 5 : *Harmless* pages 90-135

Summary

Write a summary of the events that occur in this reading section. Distinguish between the parts of the story told by Anna, Emma, and Mariah.

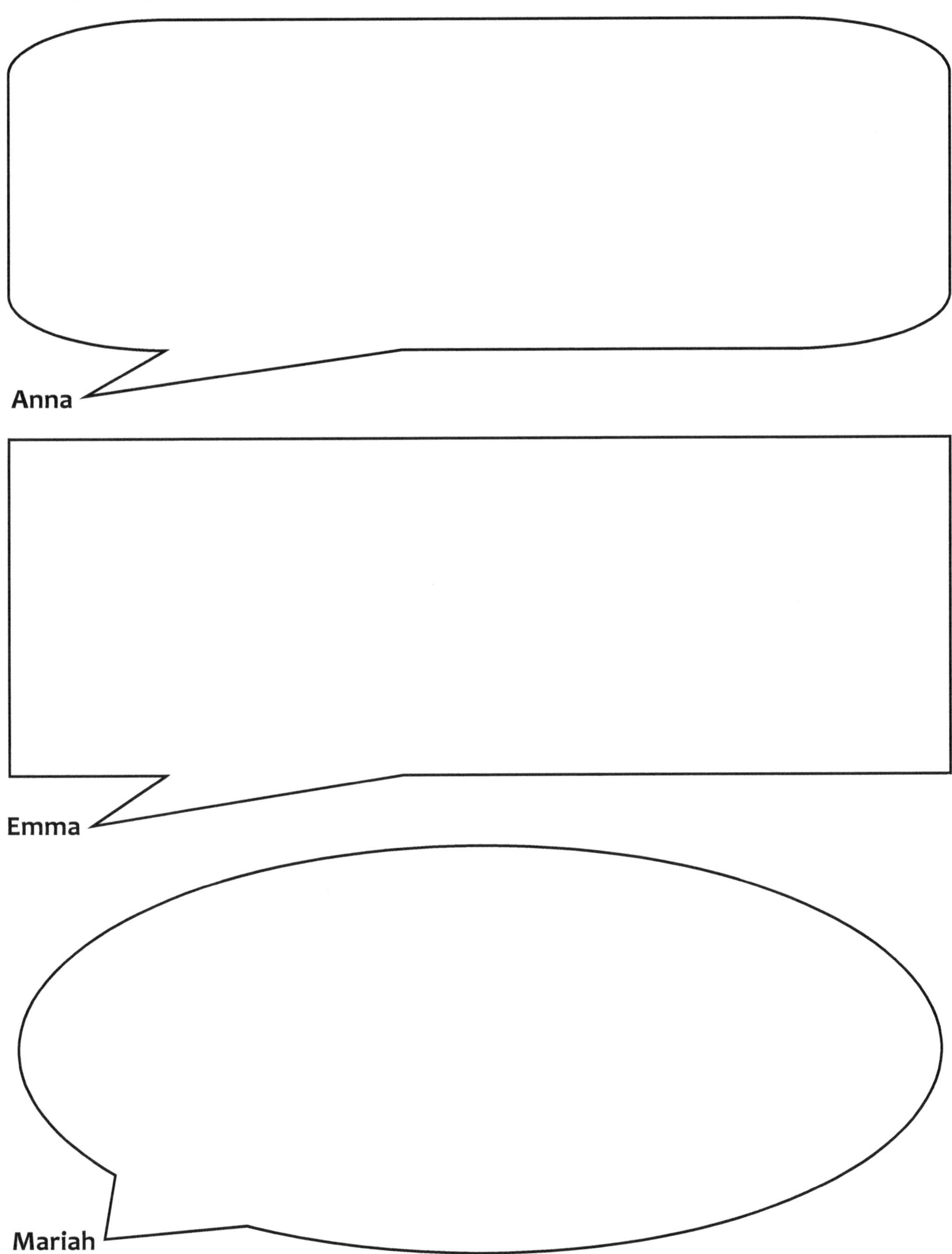

Vocabulary

Use the words from the novel printed in the cloud to complete the sentences in the box. Be careful to use the correct form of verbs, and the plural or singular form of nouns.

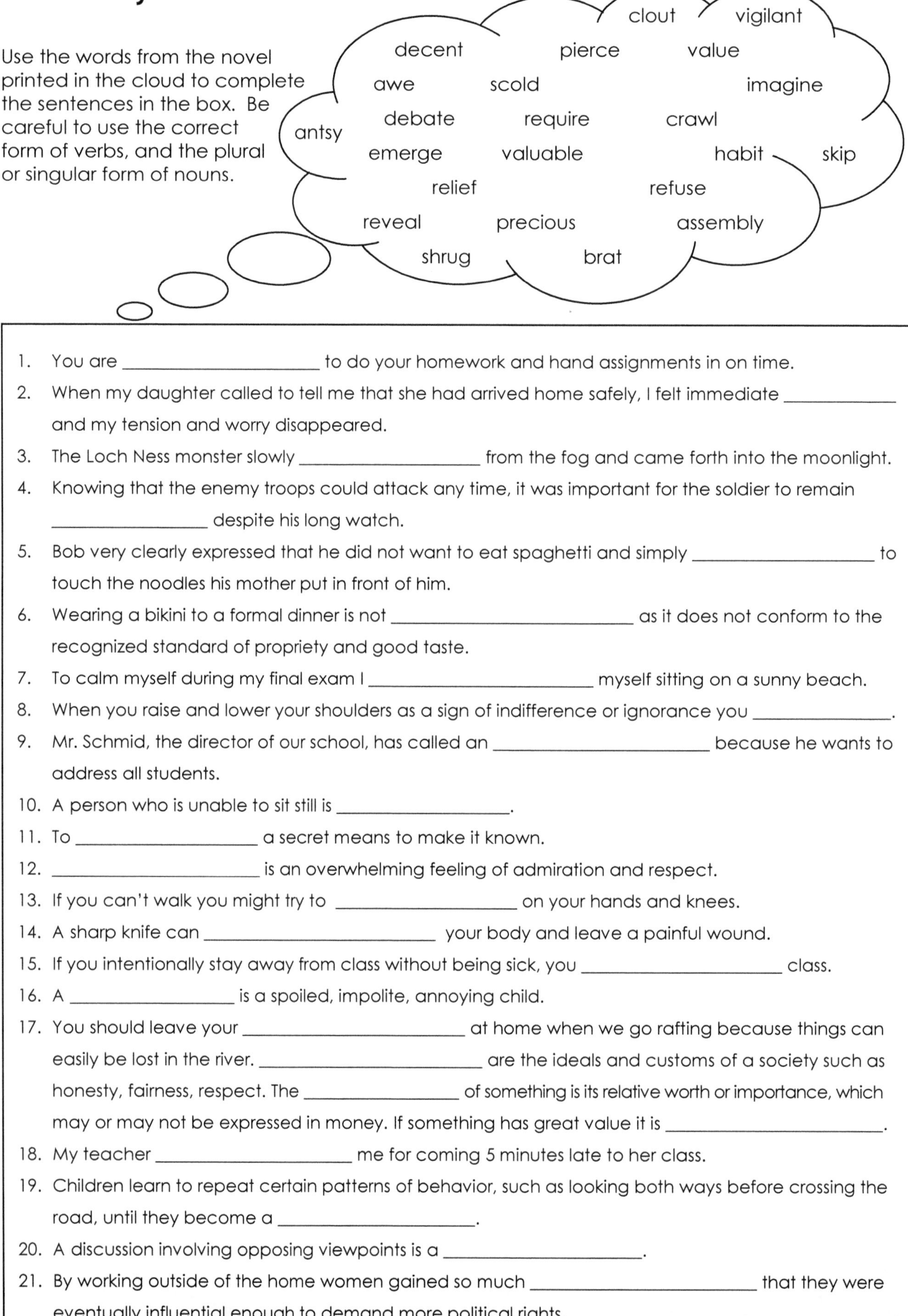

1. You are ____________________ to do your homework and hand assignments in on time.
2. When my daughter called to tell me that she had arrived home safely, I felt immediate ____________ and my tension and worry disappeared.
3. The Loch Ness monster slowly ____________________ from the fog and came forth into the moonlight.
4. Knowing that the enemy troops could attack any time, it was important for the soldier to remain _________________ despite his long watch.
5. Bob very clearly expressed that he did not want to eat spaghetti and simply ____________________ to touch the noodles his mother put in front of him.
6. Wearing a bikini to a formal dinner is not __________________________ as it does not conform to the recognized standard of propriety and good taste.
7. To calm myself during my final exam I ________________________ myself sitting on a sunny beach.
8. When you raise and lower your shoulders as a sign of indifference or ignorance you ______________.
9. Mr. Schmid, the director of our school, has called an ________________________ because he wants to address all students.
10. A person who is unable to sit still is ___________________.
11. To ____________________ a secret means to make it known.
12. ______________________ is an overwhelming feeling of admiration and respect.
13. If you can't walk you might try to ____________________ on your hands and knees.
14. A sharp knife can _________________________ your body and leave a painful wound.
15. If you intentionally stay away from class without being sick, you ______________________ class.
16. A __________________ is a spoiled, impolite, annoying child.
17. You should leave your ________________________ at home when we go rafting because things can easily be lost in the river. ________________________ are the ideals and customs of a society such as honesty, fairness, respect. The _________________ of something is its relative worth or importance, which may or may not be expressed in money. If something has great value it is ______________________.
18. My teacher ______________________ me for coming 5 minutes late to her class.
19. Children learn to repeat certain patterns of behavior, such as looking both ways before crossing the road, until they become a _____________________.
20. A discussion involving opposing viewpoints is a ______________________.
21. By working outside of the home women gained so much _________________________ that they were eventually influential enough to demand more political rights.

Vocabulary

Match these words from the novel with their definitions by writing the correct number on the line.

1. rescue
2. humble
3. pale
4. heroine
5. blink
6. remarkable
7. turmoil
8. punishment
9. tease
10. superior
11. lack
12. sophisticated
13. sulky
14. bother
15. vanish
16. haul
17. grateful
18. flimsy
19. content
20. deserve
21. caption
22. defend

___ disappear
___ satisfied with what one is or has
___ a title or explanation written for a picture in a magazine or newspaper
___ thankful
___ to playfully make fun of someone
___ gloomy and withdrawn
___ the absence of something needed or desired
___ extraordinary
___ modest
___ a state of great confusion or violent tumult
___ knowledgeable, worldly, showing education and refined taste
___ of better quality
___ to involuntarily open and close one's eyes
___ to be worthy of
___ to move by carrying or dragging
___ a whitish color, particularly of the face or skin
___ weak or ineffective
___ to save someone
___ to impose a penalty on someone
___ to ward off an attack
___ a female hero or protagonist
___ to annoy, to cause trouble

Choose seven words and write one sentence per word in which you use the word correctly and show that you have understood its meaning. Indicate the part of speech of the word as used in the sentence. Alternatively, write a ghost story in which you use at least 7 of these words correctly and indicate the part of speech of the word as used in the sentences of your story.

Example: At an auction items are sold by public outcry to the highest bidder.
(noun)

___
___
___
___
___
___
___
___
___
___
___

Questions

1. Anna is reading the story *The Scarlet Letter* in her English class. Find out who wrote that story, what it is about, and who is its protagonist. How might this famous work of American literature be connected to Anna's, Emma's, and Mariah's story?

2. On page 95 Anna attempts to express what friendship means. Try to explain her thoughts. Do you agree with her definition of friendship? How would you describe or define friendship?

3. Anna claims that Emma has changed. How?

4. Emma claims that Anna has changed. How?

5. Why do you think Emma does not want to partake in writing the article for the school newspaper?

6. With what phrase does Mariah suggest to begin the article? What does this show about her?

7. Write the article Mariah and Anna write for the school newspaper. Structure your article into 3-5 paragraphs. Include a headline and a byline. (see page 81 for information on how to write a newspaper article.)

8. What does Anna mean by "I felt a quick jab, somewhere deep in my middle, when I heard Dad say those words: *You deserve it.*"(107) ?

9. As they walk to school, what do Anna and Emma talk about?

10. How has the relationship between the three girls changed?

11. At the assembly, Emma sees the story from a new point of view. Which?

12. Who is Elinor Clements? Why are Anna and Emma so interested in her story?

13. Emma compares her mother to Ms. Malachy on page 127. What do we learn from this comparison about the relationship between Emma and her mother?

14. Is there a kind of lie that "makes you a decent person instead of a big fat liar" (132) as Mariah suggests?

15. What is the Take Back the Night march?

16. Imagine that you are either Emma, Anna, or Mariah. You do not know how to deal with your current emotions and thoughts, so you decide to write a letter to the advice columnist of a magazine. First explain your situation, next describe your thoughts, emotions, fears, desires, and finally ask for advice how to best find a solution or achieve what you want. For more information on how to write a letter, see pages 79-80.

Dear ____________________ ,

17. Read the letter of one of your classmates and write a response as if you were the advice columnist.

Section 6 : *Harmless* pages 136-197

Summary

Write a summary of the events that occur in this reading section. Distinguish between the parts of the story told by Anna, Emma, and Mariah.

Vocabulary

Use the words from the novel printed in the cloud to complete the sentences in the box. Be careful to use the correct form of verbs, and the plural or singular form of nouns.

wrinkled
recognize arrest prestigious
nag mayor
convincing distinguish frequent
pace
investigate conjure
fade except
predator mobilize charge
lurk oath

1. Before declaring war, the president instructed the minister of defense to ____________________ the troops: the soldiers had to be organized, well-prepared, and ready for action.
2. The head of government of a city or town is the ____________________.
3. A policeman was sent to ____________________ the disappearance of some property from a hotel. When he arrived, he found that the hotel staff had caught a boy in one of the rooms with a camera and some cash that did not belong to him. The policeman ____________________ the boy, and brought him to the police station. At the police station the boy could not give a satisfactory explanation for his actions and the police decided to ____________________ him with the theft of the camera and cash.
4. I had not seen Marco for 10 years, so when I met him again at a party I did not ____________________ him until he introduced himself to me.
5. Everyone came to class on time ____________________ me because the cable car doors would not open and I was stuck for about 15 minutes.
6. Because I had slept in my suit it was very ____________________ in the morning.
7. An animal that lives by attacking, capturing, and eating other animals is a ____________________.
8. The twins looked so alike that I could not ____________________ one from the other.
9. Due to our preference for Italian food, we ____________________ the restaurant *Mamma Leone*. We go there every Saturday and sometimes even during the week.
10. The salesman gave such a ____________________ demonstration of the car's safety features that I decided to buy it on the spot.
11. Being nervous and unable to sit still, Edgar ____________________ up and down the hallway while the surgeons were giving his wife a heart-transplant.
12. My mother is always ____________________ me with her annoying demands to clean up my room.
13. The moment she started speaking about her ex-boyfriend he showed up as if called into existence by magic. It was as if she had ____________________ him just by mentioning his name.
14. The cat was ____________________ patiently in the bush intending to catch a bird once it sat down on a branch.
15. Before testifying in court, witnesses have to take an ____________________ that they will tell the truth and nothing but the truth so help them God.
16. When flowers lose freshness and vividness of color they ____________________.
17. Stanford is one of the most ____________________ universities in California: it has a reputation for being one of the best schools in the world.

Vocabulary

Use the words from the novel printed in the cloud to complete the sentences in the box. Be careful to use the correct form of verbs, and the plural or singular form of nouns.

apart, purr, promotion, on purpose, bruise, choke, drown, hug, vagrant, chant, scar, haunt, shelter, weigh, delighted, crowd, malleable, tamper, participate, glare, empathetic, surrender, anticipate, faculty

1. Before reaching a decision, Marta carefully ______________________ all facts and arguments that spoke for or against that decision.
2. This old castle is ______________________ by the ghost of my great-great-grandmother who was murdered and will not come to rest.
3. During the storm, Lynn took ____________________ in a cave he found by following a herd of sheep.
4. When you experience great pleasure or joy you are ______________________.
5. The star boxer ____________________________ every one of his opponent's moves and was never surprised by a punch.
6. Before saying goodbye Nils ______________________ Lilo and held her close for a long time.
7. After my boxing match with Robin, I had so many _________________________ that I looked like a blue-green spotted giraffe.
8. When wounds heal they sometimes leave a _______________________ on the skin.
9. A child's mind is very _________________________, it can be easily influenced or shaped, which is why many parents are very careful what they let their children watch on TV.
10. New York and Sydney are thousands of miles ______________________________.
11. A counselor should be __________________________ and show sensitivity and comprehension for the situation of others.
12. I am not going to apologize for breaking your computer because I did it _______________________. Breaking it seemed the only way to get you away from it and start talking to me!
13. Understanding that they were outnumbered, the soldiers waved a white flag and ____________________ to the Maori warriors under the condition that they would not be killed.
14. When a cat is comfortable and wants to show its pleasure it ________________________.
15. A piece of food was stuck in his windpipe so he nearly _______________________.
16. It is a criminal act to _____________________ with official records in order to change or falsify them.
17. A person who wanders around, has no permanent home or place of employment, and often begs money to support himself is a ______________________.
18. Why are you ________________ at me? Have I done anything to deserve your angry, piercing stare?
19. It is compulsory at our school that you ______________________ in a sports activity.
20. The entire teaching and administrative force of a school or university is its ____________________.
21. A large number of people gathered closely together is a ____________________.
22. Because Farhad could not swim and tried to breathe under water he ______________________.
23. _________________________ the slogan "Obama for President", the crowd of enthusiastic supporters marched through town.
24. The employee was proud to receive a ___________________________ from assistant to team leader.

Vocabulary

Match these words from the novel with their definitions by writing the correct number on the line. Choose seven words and write one sentence per word in which you use the word correctly and show that you have understood its meaning. Indicate the part of speech of the word as used in the sentence.

1. evidence
2. pine
3. resemble
4. tide
5. treacherous
6. affection
7. award
8. interfere
9. harrass
10. mention
11. tumble
12. assault
13. preserve
14. slide
15. vow
16. infinite

___ a sudden violent attack
___ love or strong positive emotion
___ immeasurably great, endless
___ a prize
___ deceptive, unstable, risky, unreliable
___ to keep safe from injury or decay
___ the periodic rise and fall of the ocean caused by gravitational forces of the sun and moon
___ to meddle, to come between, to work against
___ to move by slipping or skidding
___ to speak of
___ to be alike, to be similar to
___ proof, something that helps reach a conclusion or make something clear
___ a serious promise
___ to disturb, irritate, attack, annoy persistently
___ an evergreen tree with needle-shaped leaves
___ to fall helplessly, to lose one's footing

Questions

1. What does Emma's statement "Unfortunately, there isn't anything I'm forgetting" (139) suggest?

2. Why does Emma compare Ellie's family to Wile E. Coyote?

3. How has the relationship between Emma and Silas changed?

4. What does Mariah do on the evening of the march? Why do you think she did not attend the march?

5. What does Mariah realize about herself on the evening of the march? How does this make her feel?

6. Why does Carl forbid Mariah to spend time with Anna?

7. Would you ever forbid your child to spend time with someone and for what reason?

8. Who does the police arrest for assaulting the three girls? What evidence do they have?

9. How does Detective Caputo "help" the girls identify the man? Do you think he was right to do so?

10. Emma attempts to describe her emotions by saying "I just felt that white expanse of nothingness slowly spreading to the edges of me"(157). What does she mean?

11. Three things keep Mariah from telling Detective Stevens the truth. Which?

12. What does Emma mean by "But no matter how soundly you build your sand castle, there are still things like wind and rain and the tide that will break these bridges apart, and in time, your sand castle will fall" (171).

13. Mariah says that she "felt divided in two"(177). Which two persons does she think she is? Explain.

14. Why does Anna not feel guilty about the arrest?

15. This is the front page of the *Riverbend Gazette*, the town's newspaper, on the day after David Allen's arrest. Complete the sections with writing or photos (newspaper-cut-outs or drawings).

Today's Features:

(PRICE)

RIVERBEND GAZETTE

(SLOGAN OF NEWSPAPER)

Today's Features:

(DATE)

(HEADLINE)

PHOTO

CAPTION:

PHOTO

CAPTION:

(HEADLINE)

Inside:
(SECTIONS, PAGE NO., BRIEF SUMMARY)

Sports:

Local Events:

Weather:

16. Which summer job does Mariah really want? Why do you think she wants that type of work?

17. What do you think of the relationship between Anna and Tobey? In what way is it similar to other boy-girl relationships we have encountered in the novel?

18. Emma and her father spend the day together. Where do they go? What does this show about their personalities? How is this outing different from previous such outings?

19. How does Emma interpret the road sign "Soft Shoulder Ahead" ? What does it really mean?

20. Choose one of the following writing tasks and write it in the space provided.

    A. Write the letter Mariah might write to Detective Scott telling the truth.
    B. Write the letter Anna might write to Detective Scott telling the truth.
    C. Write the letter Emma might write to Detective Scott telling the truth.
    D. Write an interview with David Allen to be published in the *Riverbend Gazette*.

21. What bothers Detective Scott about David Allen?

22. Mariah believes she could tell Silas the truth on one condition. What is that condition and why would she tell him under those circumstances? What does this show about Mariah?

23. What is Mariah's attitude towards the river? How does this correspond with the story?

24. Why might Silas think he is "a wreck" (196)?

25. Write this chapter from Silas' perspective. OR: Write the diary entry Silas might write that evening.

Section 7 : *Harmless* pages 198-229

Summary

Write a summary of the events that occur in this reading section. Distinguish between the parts of the story told by Anna, Emma, and Mariah.

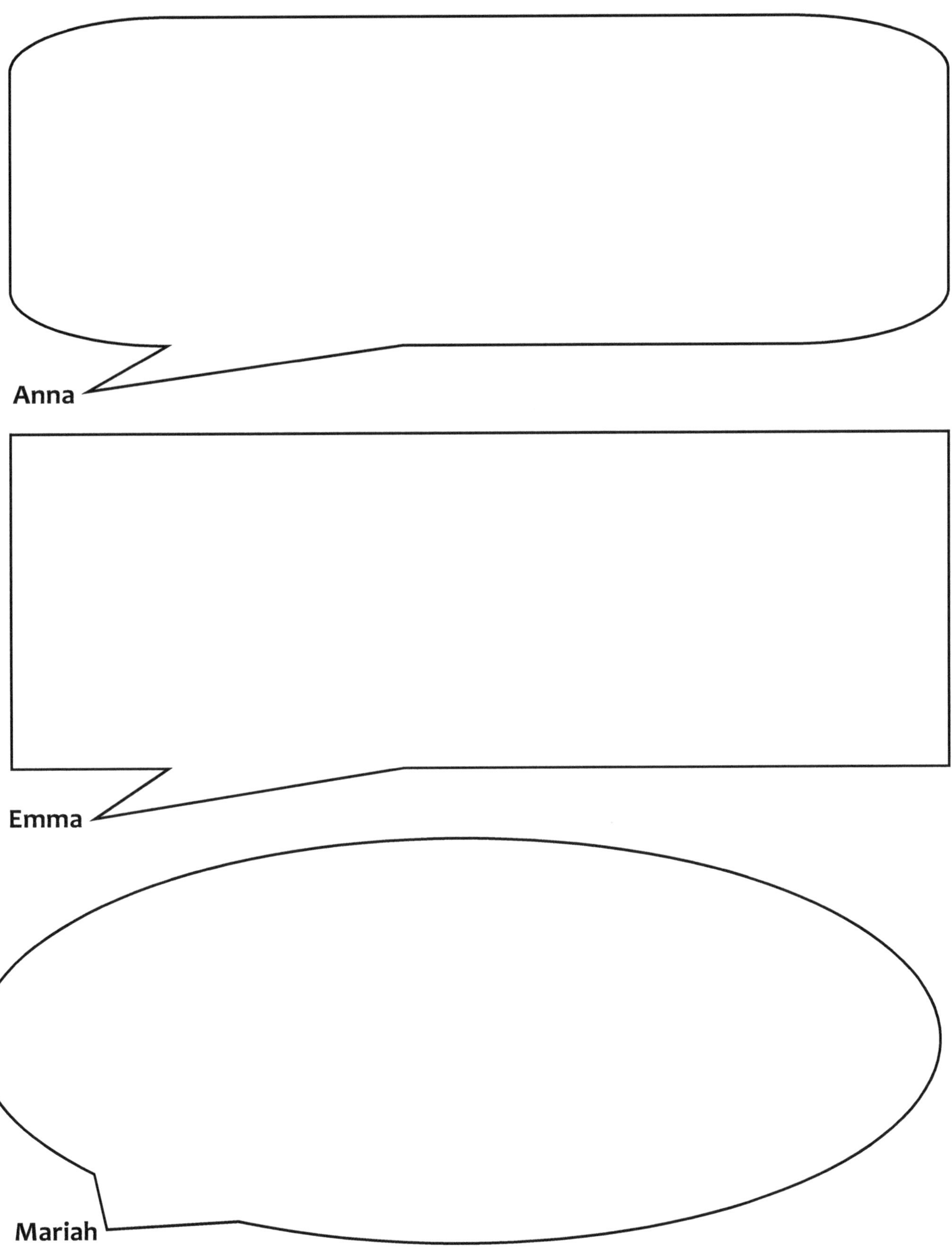

Vocabulary

Determine the part of speech of the words from the novel printed in the cloud. Use these words or one of their parts of speech to complete the sentences in the box. Be careful to use the correct form of verbs, and the plural or singular form of nouns.

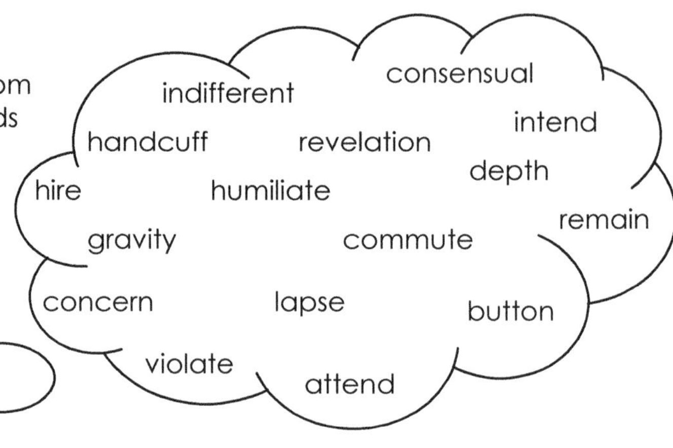

1. It takes Aliya 40 minutes to get from her home to her workplace. She ____________________ every morning and evening by train.
2. Although fully bilingual, the teacher just could not think of the translation of the word *mute*. This __________________ of memory annoyed him so much that he marched out of the classroom and looked up the word in a dictionary in the library.
3. Students who do not ______________________ more than 20% of their classes will be expelled.
4. Although he knew he had only a few weeks to live, he tried to ignore the ________________ of his illness and appeared as cheerful as ever.
5. When two or more people willingly participate in an action the action is _________________.
6. Because Richard resisted arrest, the policeman used ______________________ to restrain his arms behind his back.
7. After 300 years, the only thing that _______________________ of the once magnificent palace is one crumbling wall.
8. By smoking in the dining hall Max ____________________ the houserules.
9. We were all shocked when we heard that three students had died on their schooltrip, only Tony was completely ______________________: he did not care at all about what had happened.
10. The principal will have to __________________ more teachers because the number of students at our school has increased.
11. Isabel _____________________ her colleague by making fun of his clothing in front of the principal and the students.
12. Some very strange fish live in the _________________ of the ocean.
13. Finding out about her husband cheating on her with his secretary was a terrible ____________________ for Yvonne because she had not realized that their marriage was in trouble at all.
14. The teacher ________________________ to give us a test about the novel we are reading.
15. Global warming is an issue that _____________________ us all.
16. A __________________ on my blouse came off so I cannot close it. Could you please sew it back on?

Match these words from the novel with their definitions by writing the correct number on the line. Choose five words and write one sentence per word in which you use the word correctly and show that you have understood its meaning. Indicate the part of speech of the word as used in the sentence.

1. minor
2. inseparable
3. fabric
4. amaze
5. expel
6. reverse
7. principled
8. weep
9. retrieve
10. urgency
11. ruin
12. void

___ to surprise and overwhelm with wonder
___ destroy
___ move backward
___ to regain, get back, save, repair
___ empty space, nothingness
___ cry, shed tears
___ a cloth made by weaving or knitting fibers
___ something of pressing importance
___ something that cannot be taken apart
___ a person under the legal age of full responsibility
___ have high moral or ethical standards
___ force to leave, throw out, kick out

Questions

1. Why is Anna angry at her mother?

2. What does Anna mean by "It would be another death. Another loss. Another miscarriage"(201) ?

3. What makes Emma decide to tell the truth?

4. Who is the first person Emma tells the truth?

5. How does Emma describe her feelings after she has told the truth? What does this mean?

6. How does David Allen react?

7. How are the girls punished?

8. Why does Emma decide to return to her old high school? Would you have done the same thing? Explain.

9. What do the "new lives" the girls choose tell about their personality, how they have grown up, what they have learned from their deeds?

10. Why do you think the girls were arrested in class and handcuffed?

11. What does Emma want to suggest by calling her brother "Silas Devastaticus" (222) ?

12. How does Emma come to think of what happened between her and Owen?

13. How does each girl deal with the consequences after the truth is out? What does this tell about the personality of each girl?

14. Which girl do you like best, which do you like the least and why? Write a 3-paragraph essay in which you compare/contrast your likes and dislikes of the three protagonists.

Additional Writing and Creative Tasks

1. Design and write the newspaper front page for the day after the truth comes out. Use an A3 sheet of paper.

2. Write the letter of apology one of the girls might write to David Allen.

3. Write or act out the conversation one of the girls might have with her parents on the evening the truth came out.

4. Write a review of the novel.

5. Imagine you could interview the author of this novel. Prepare a set of questions to ask the author.

5a. With a classmate, act out the interview with the author.

5b. Give your set of questions to a classmate and have him/her answer the questions in writing as if s/he were the author.

5c. Write your own responses to your questions as if you were the author.

5d. Try to contact the author at info@danareinhardt.net and ask her politely to respond to your questions. If she does, write up the interview as you would for a magazine article.

6. Create a collage of quotes (with page references!) that reflect the essence of this novel.

7. Create a character collage: write out quotes, cut out words and pictures from magazines, internet, etc. that fit and describe one character in the novel.

8. Write an essay comparing / contrasting the three main characters.

9. Three years have passed since that day the truth came out. The three girls have graduated from their respective high schools and are about to start college. Coincidentally, they have all chosen to go to the same college and, by luck of the draw, end up being roommates. This is their first meeting and conversation since that day three years ago. Capture this new chapter in their lives and the conversation they might have in writing.

10. Create a quiz or board game about this novel.

11. Imagine the three girls are invited to a talk show in which the host tries to have the conflicts between the girls flare up for the entertainment of the audience. For this purpose she might also call other guests from the novel. Prepare the talk show as a role-play activity and act it out in class.

The Characters

Fill in the venn diagram below by giving information about the characters you learn from the novel. Use quotes by and about them to back up your claims.

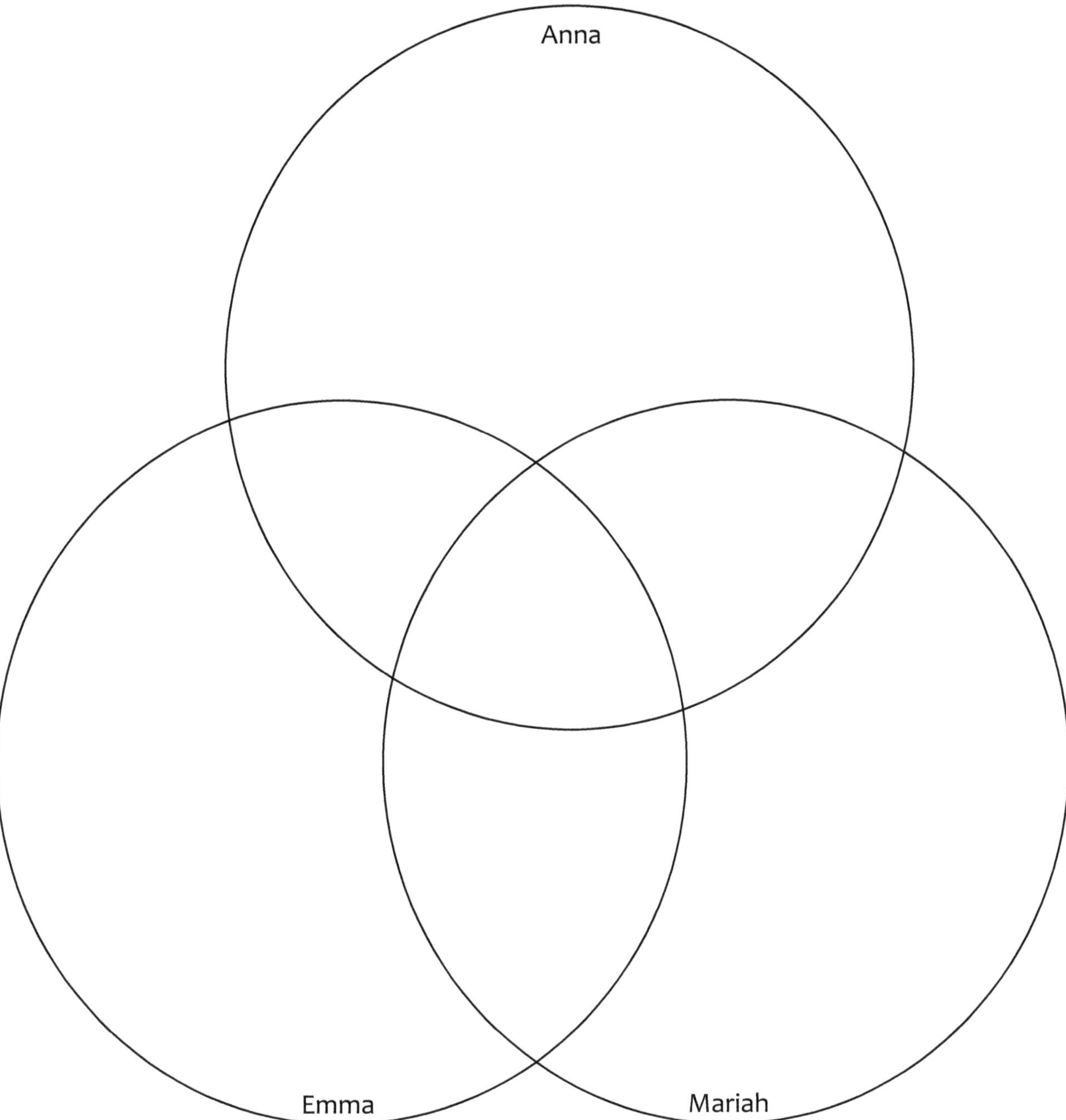

Foils are characters who through strong contrast enhance distinctive characteristics of another character. To what extent are Anna, Emma, and Mariah foils for each other? Are there other characters in the novel who function as foils for other characters? Which?

Dynamic Characters

Explain how the three main characters change and what causes them to change. Write the causes of change into the lightning bolts; how they change into the boxes.

Relationships and Conflicts Chart

By completing the chart below, explore the relationships and conflicts between characters. Use different colors to draw arrows and lines explaining conflicts and relationships.

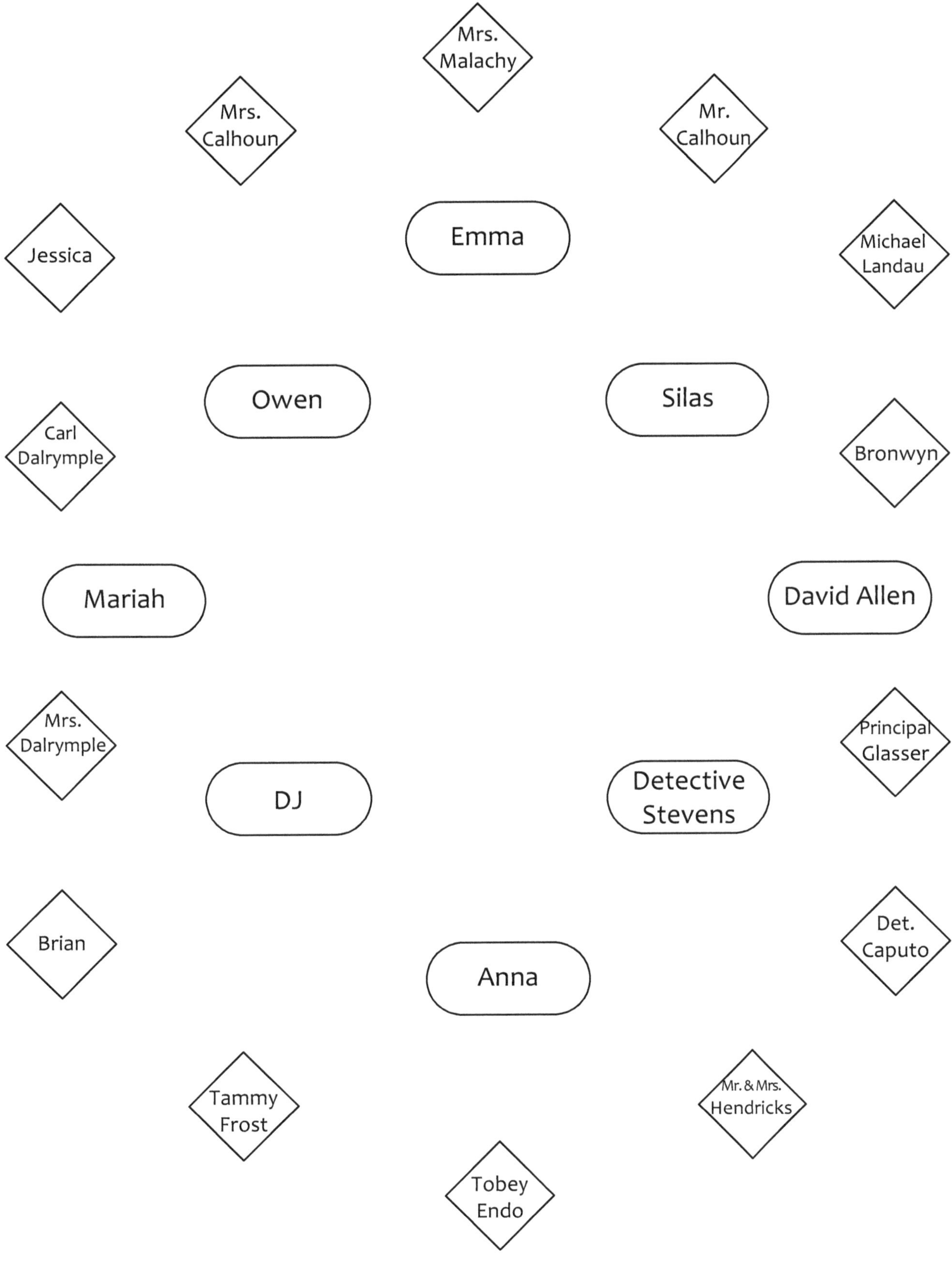

Conflict Analysis

Choose three conflicts from your conflict chart above and analyze them in more detail. State their origin, what exacerbates them, and their resolution. If there is no resolution, indicate this by stating "unresolved".

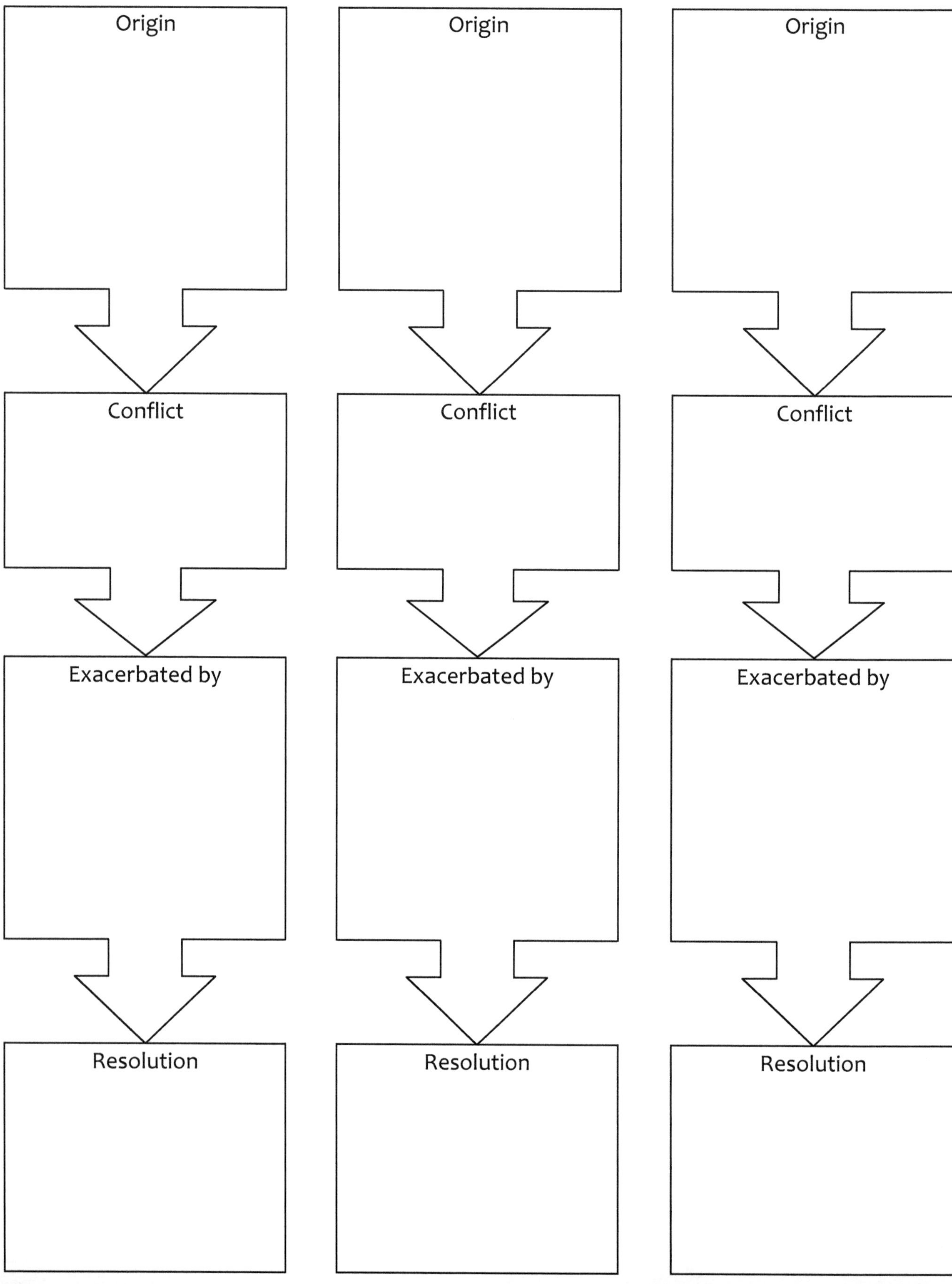

Character Types

Place each character from the novel in one or more of the character-type-boxes below. Justify why you think each character belongs in the respective box. Add two character-types of your own.

Victims	Deceivers	Innocents

Guilty	Righteous	Troublemakers

Doers	Followers	Doubters

Have good intentions		

How to Write a Formal Letter

When writing a formal letter you must follow specific formatting, punctuation, and wording requirements. Read the information below to learn more about writing this text type.

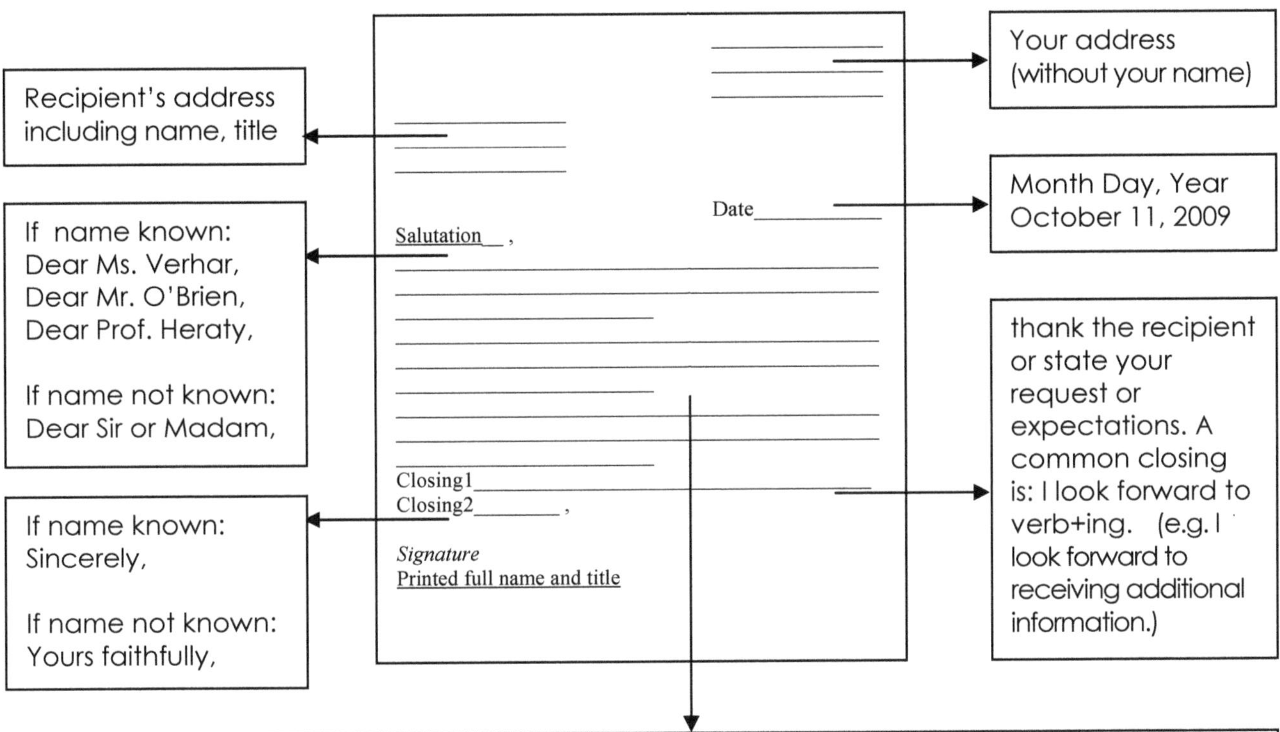

In the first lines of your letter, clearly state your intention or purpose for writing. Always be polite (even in a letter of complaint!), use complete sentences with correct punctuation, structure your letter in paragraphs, try to use formal vocabulary, do not use short verb forms (can't = cannot, don't = do not, he's = he is, aren't = are not, etc.) and do not use exclamation marks (!).

How to Write an Informal Letter

When writing an informal letter you are freer than when writing a formal one, but you must still follow certain rules. Keep in mind that informal letters can range from very informal to semi-formal. An informal letter that you write to a very close friend who is the same age as you will use different wording and structure than an informal letter you write to your grandmother thanking her for a birthday present, or an informal letter you write to a colleague or superior. Read the information below to learn more about writing this text type.

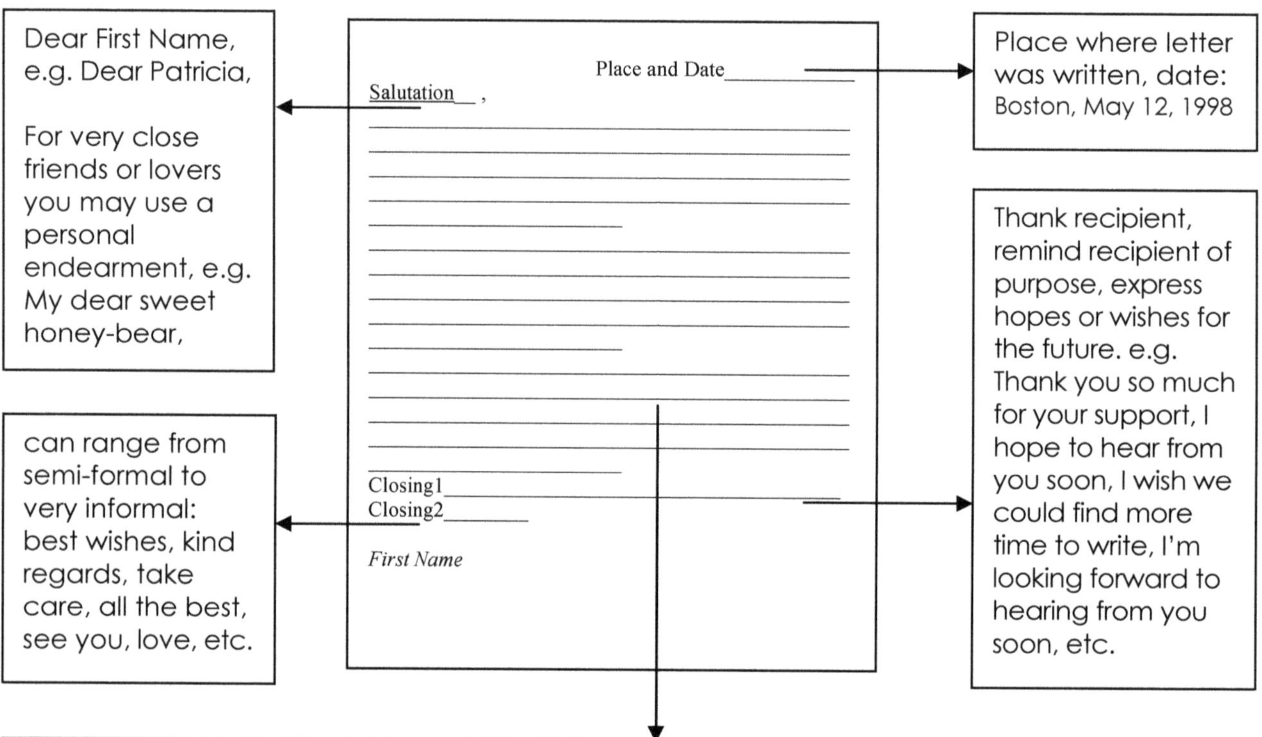

Depending on how well you know the recipient and how informal your letter is, you may use very informal expressions, short verb forms, abbreviations, colloquialisms, make references to mutual knowledge, shared experiences, express opinions about friends, colleagues, events, be personal and show emotion (enthusiasm, anger, sadness, etc.). Your letter to a close friend need not be structured in paragraphs, but it makes it easier to read. Writing to a very close friend also allows you to use stream-of-consciousness technique in which you just write whatever pops into your head and jump from one topic to another. You may further ask for feedback with expressions such as "right?", "don't you agree?", or "what do you think?", and use exclamation marks for effect. A semi-formal letter on the other hand will try to keep emotions, colloquialisms and abbreviations to a minimum (unless they are work-related argot), and use paragraph structure and more formal phrases, salutations, closings, and should be signed with your first and last name.

How to Write a Newspaper Article

Read the information below to learn more about writing this text type.

Large-sized lettering to attract reader's attention, e.g. Switzerland wins World Cup. Headlines use mainly present tense (even for past events), leave out articles and auxiliary verbs, and use *to* for future tenses, e.g. Marc Forster to film at Institut Montana; Tsunami leaves thousands dead.

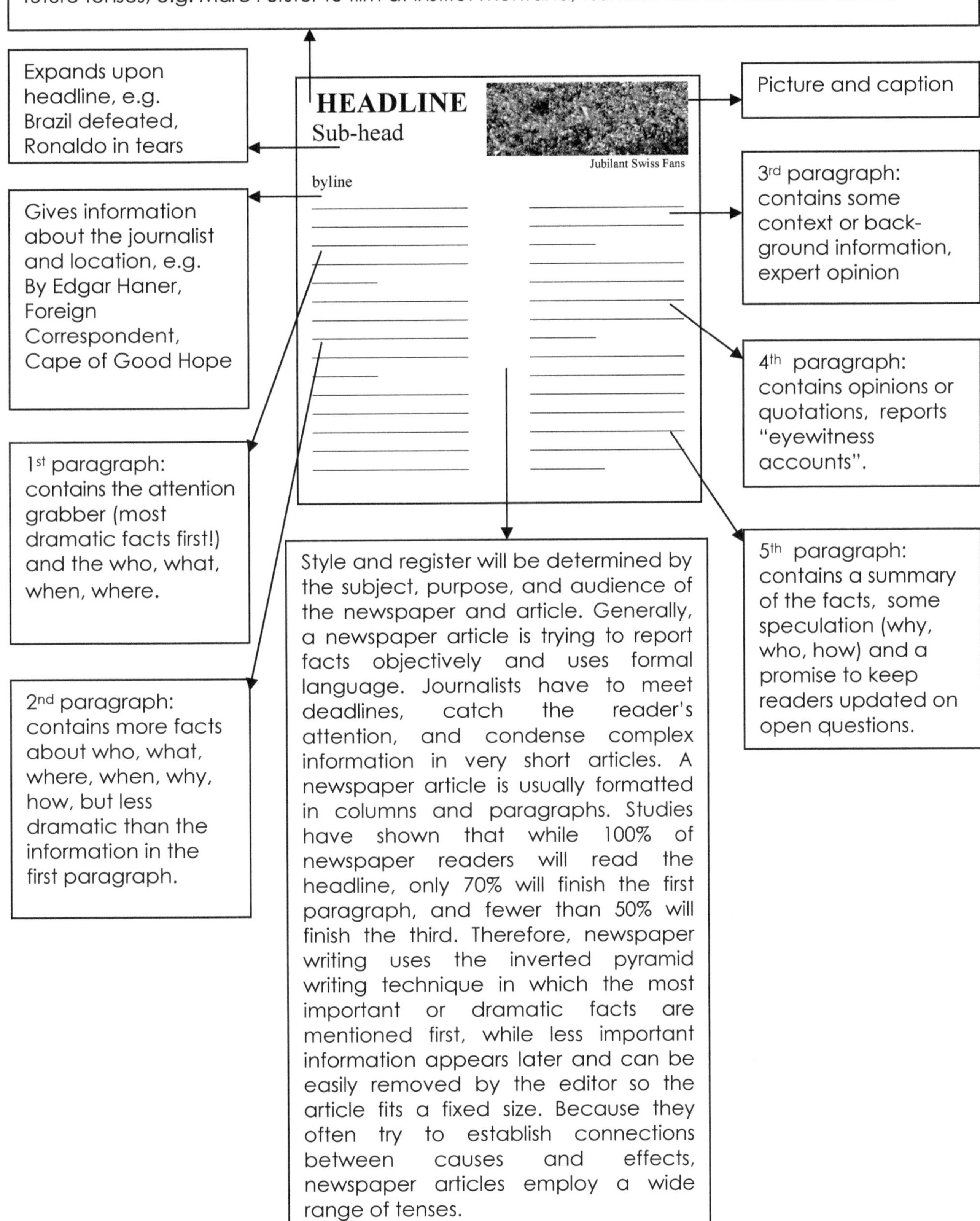

www.ingramcontent.com/pod-product-compliance
Ingram Content Group UK Ltd.
Pitfield, Milton Keynes, MK11 3LW, UK
UKHW061817190726
13853UKWH00006B/2203

9 783033 022133